MACMILLAN READER
PRE-INTERMEDIATE LEVEL

H. G. WELLS

The Invisible Man

Retold by Nick Bullard

520 683 60 5

PRE-INTERMEDIATE LEVEL

Founding Editor: John Milne

The Macmillan Readers provide a choice of enjoyable reading materials for learners of English. The series is published at six levels – Starter, Beginner, Elementary, Pre-intermediate, Intermediate and Upper.

Level Control

Information, structure and vocabulary are controlled to suit the students' ability at each level.

The number of words at each level:

Starter	about 300 basic words
Beginner	about 600 basic words
Elementary	about 1100 basic words
Pre-intermediate	about 1400 basic words
Intermediate	about 1600 basic words
Upper	about 2200 basic words

Vocabulary

Some difficult words and phrases in this book are important for understanding the story. Some of these words are explained in the story, some are shown in the pictures, and others are marked with a number like this: ...[3]. Phrases are marked with [P]. Words with a number are explained in the *Glossary* at the end of the book and phrases are explained on the *Useful Phrases* page.

Answer Keys

Answer Keys for the *Points For Understanding* and *Exercises* sections can be found at www.macmillanenglish.com/readers.

Contents

A Note About The Author

Herbert George Wells was born near London in 1866. He was the youngest of four children. His parents had a small shop, but it was not a successful business and they never had very much money.

When he was eleven, Wells had an accident and broke his leg. He had to stay in bed and his father brought him books from the local library. The books helped him to escape into other worlds and lives, and helped him to decide that he wanted to be a writer. When he was thirteen, Wells had to leave school and find work because his parents had very little money. For three years he worked in a department store[1] in Southsea, on the south coast of England. He hated the work, but it was useful to him in his later writing, as we can see in the chapter on the department store in *The Invisible Man*.

In 1883, Wells got a job as an assistant teacher in a school. As well as teaching, he was able to prepare for exams. In September 1884, he went to study at the Normal School of Science in London. He was not a good student at first, and he left without a degree[2]. But, after returning to teaching again, he finally got a degree in Zoology from the University of London in 1890. He started teaching biology and his first published book was *A Textbook of Biology*. Then he became ill and had to stop teaching. He had to begin to write professionally.

At first he wrote for newspapers and magazines, then in 1895 he published *The Time Machine*, his first novel. This was very successful, and it was followed by a number of other popular books. They included *The Invisible Man* (1897), *The War of the Worlds* (1898), and *The First Men in the Moon* (1901). Wells was always interested in science. His first books were all science fiction[3], and he tried to base[4] the science in them on fact. In *The Invisible Man*, for example, he gave a

4

scientific explanation of the invisibility[5]. By 1900 his books were popular all over the English-speaking world. They were also translated into a number of other languages.

As a scientist, Wells was very excited by new scientific inventions[6]. The invention of the radio gave him a new way to explain his ideas. His voice was often heard on the radio in the 1930s and 1940s, mostly[7] talking about scientific progress[8]. He died in London in 1946.

A Note About The Story

When it was published in 1897, *The Invisible Man* was a truly modern story. It took the progress in science at the end of the nineteenth century as a starting point. With science, anything seemed possible, even the idea of an invisible person. Wells did not want Griffin's invisibility to be magic, and he is very careful to describe some of the science that makes it possible. For this reason the two main characters in the story, Griffin (the Invisible Man) and Dr Kemp, are both scientists. At this time scientists often worked alone, and at home, and both Griffin and Dr Kemp do this. Dr Kemp is clearly a rich man and can pay for his research[9]. But Griffin is not, and money is a problem for him.

The story is set in the last years of the nineteenth century and takes place partly in London and mostly in Sussex near the south coast of England. Iping is real village, but Port Burdock and Port Stowe are not real places. Port Burdock is probably Southsea, where Wells worked for three years as a boy. London is shown as the busy, dirty, city that it was in the 1890s.

Wells clearly thought a lot about the good and bad points of invisibility. These are shown in particular in the London chapters when Griffin has just become invisible. When Griffin is first invisible, his problems can make us laugh, but as the story moves on they become more and more serious.

The Invisible Man was first made into a film in 1933. There have been many other adaptations[10] since that date.

The People In The Story

Griffin –
the Invisible Man

Dr Kemp

Mrs Hall

Mr Marvel

Dr Cuss

Colonel Adye

1

The Arrival of the Strange Man

The stranger arrived early in February, on a day of cold wind and snow. He walked over the hill from Bramblehurst railway station, carrying[11] a small bag. He was wearing black gloves[12], and a long coat, and he was covered from head to foot. His hat hid his face and you could only see the shiny[13], pink end of his nose. He threw open the front door of the Coach and Horses, and walked in.

'A fire!' he called, 'And quickly, please. A room and a fire!'

He followed the landlady[14] Mrs Hall into the guests' lounge, paid her the two pounds she asked for, and sat down. Mrs Hall started to light[15] the fire.

Mrs Hall left him by the fire and went to the kitchen to cook him a meal. This stranger was excellent news for her. Visitors were rare in the village of Iping in winter, and visitors with money were rare at any time. She started her cooking and then picked up some plates and a glass and carried them through to the table in the guests' lounge. The fire was burning brightly and she was surprised to see that her visitor was still wearing his coat and hat. He was standing by the window with his back to her, and he was watching the snow falling in the garden.

'Can I take your hat and coat, sir?' she asked. 'I can put them to dry in the kitchen.'

'No,' the stranger answered, 'I prefer to keep them on.'

He turned to look at her, and she saw that he was wearing dark glasses. He had a thick beard[16] and she could not see his face at all.

'As you like, sir,' she answered.

He did not answer, and he turned his face away again. She finished with the table. She left the room, and returned to

'A fire!' he called, 'And quickly, please. A room and a fire!'

the kitchen. When she came back with his food he was still looking out of the window.

'Your lunch is ready, sir,' said Mrs Hall.

'Thank you,' answered the stranger.

She left, closing the door. But when she got back to the kitchen, she saw that she had forgotten the bread. She picked up the bread and returned to the lounge. She knocked[17] on the door, and walked straight in. The stranger moved quickly and she saw something white. She put down the bread and then saw that his wet coat and hat were on a chair by the fire. His wet boots were standing beside them.

'I'll take these now, to dry,' said Mrs Hall, and she started to pick them up.

'Leave the hat!' he said suddenly, and she turned to look at him. For a moment she was too surprised to speak. He was holding a white handkerchief[18] over his mouth. But what really surprised Mrs Hall was the bandage[19]. It covered all of his face above his dark glasses. Another bandage covered his ears. All she could see of him was the end of his shiny pink nose. He was wearing a dark brown jacket which covered him up to his neck, and she could see beard and hair between the bandages and the jacket.

He was still wearing gloves, and was holding a handkerchief in front of his mouth. 'Leave the hat!' he said again.

Nervously she put the hat back on the chair. 'I didn't know,' she began, 'that ...' and she stopped, embarrassed[20].

'Thank you,' he said, and he looked at the door, and then back at her.

'They'll be dry soon,' she said, and left the room with his coat and boots.

The visitor sat for a moment without moving. He looked across at the window, stood up, and walked over to close the curtains[21]. The room was now almost dark. He returned to the table and continued eating.

'He's had an accident or something, poor man,' Mrs Hall said to herself in the kitchen. 'And those dark glasses. And the handkerchief in front of his mouth. Perhaps he's hurt[22] his mouth as well.'

A few minutes later Mrs Hall returned to the lounge to clear the table. The stranger was sitting by the fire and seemed to be more relaxed[23]. But his mouth was still covered.

'I have left some bags and boxes at Bramblehurst station,' he said. 'Can somebody go and get them for me?'

'We can get them for you tomorrow, sir,' she answered.

'Could somebody get them for me today?' he asked.

'I don't think so, sir. There's a lot of snow. Last year my sister's son had an accident in the snow on that road. He hurt his head very badly. He had to wear a lot of bandages, and my sister helped him to take them on and off every day.' Mrs Hall looked at him closely. 'Sir, if—'

'Thank you,' said the visitor. And he turned away.

Mrs Hall was angry with the stranger. But then she remembered the money. She left the room and returned quietly to the kitchen.

The stranger stayed in the lounge until four o'clock. He sat by the fire and the room grew darker and darker.

———

At four o'clock in the afternoon, Teddy Henfrey came into the Coach and Horses.

'Good evening, Teddy,' said Mrs Hall. 'I'm glad you're here. We've got a problem with the clock in the guests' lounge. The minute hand is fine, but the hour hand doesn't move. It just sits on six. Could you look at it? I know you're good with clocks.'

'Certainly[24],' said Teddy, and he followed her to the lounge.

The stranger was sitting in the armchair by the fire, and seemed to be asleep. The only light in the room came from the fire, so the room was dark and red. For a moment it seemed to Mrs Hall that the stranger had a very big mouth. It was wide open and seemed to take up all the bottom of his face. Then the stranger woke up, and his hand, with the handkerchief, went up to his mouth.

'Excuse me, sir,' she said. 'This man needs to look at the clock in this room.'

'Look at the clock?' he answered. 'Certainly.'

Mrs Hall went to get a lamp, and the visitor stood up. When she returned with the lamp, and the room was brighter, Teddy Henfrey was surprised to see the big dark glasses and the white bandages.

The stranger turned to Mrs Hall. 'I'm glad that someone is going to look at the clock,' he said. 'But usually I don't want people coming into this room. Have my things arrived?'

'Tomorrow morning, sir,' answered Mrs Hall.

'I must explain,' continued the stranger. 'I'm a scientist. I need to do some experiments[25], and everything I need is in my boxes. It's important that I can do my experiments alone, and that nobody comes into the room. Also, I have had an accident and I have to be very careful with my eyes. Sometimes I need to be in the dark. I hope you understand. That will be all,' and he turned away.

Mrs Hall left the room. 'I was right about the accident,' she thought. But really, this visitor was not very polite.

Teddy started to work on the clock. He took off the minute hand and the hour hand. He saw the problem immediately[26], but he wanted to talk to this stranger, so he started to push at things inside the clock. The stranger just stood and watched him with his big eyes and bandaged face.

'Cold today, isn't it?' Teddy said.

'Why don't you just finish?' said the stranger, angrily. 'You just need to fix the hour hand. You're playing.'

'Certainly, sir,' said Teddy. 'Oh yes, I see the problem now.' He fixed the two hands back quickly, packed up his things and went. He walked back through the village feeling angry with the stranger. He turned a corner and met Mrs Hall's husband, on his way home.

'Good evening Teddy,' said Mr Hall.

'Good evening,' answered Teddy. 'You've got a strange man staying with you at the Coach and Horses.' He told Mr Hall about the visitor. 'I think he's hiding something,' Teddy continued. 'Perhaps the police are after him. I certainly wouldn't want a man like that staying in my house.' And he walked off into the night.

When he arrived home, Mr Hall tried to discuss the stranger with his wife. But she did not want to listen. She was worried about the stranger, too, but he had money, and that was the most important thing.

2

One Thousand and One Bottles

The stranger's bags and boxes arrived in Iping the next day by horse and cart[27]. There were bags of clothes, and there was also a big box of books – fat books with strange writing. And there were at least ten boxes of glass bottles. Mr Hall stood outside the Coach and Horses talking to the driver of the cart. He was also looking with interest at the bags and boxes. The stranger was getting impatient, so he came outside dressed in his coat, hat and gloves. He did not see the carter's dog under the cart.

'Can you get my boxes in quickly?' he said. 'I've been waiting for a long time.' He walked to the back of the cart and picked up one of the smaller boxes.

The dog did not like this. He jumped up at the stranger, biting first his hand, and then the leg of his trousers.

'Lie down!' shouted the carter to his dog. Then he jumped down from his cart and pulled the dog away. The stranger looked down at his glove and his trousers, and then ran back inside and went to his room.

'It bit him!' said Mr Hall. 'I must go and see if he's all right.' He ran inside and up the stairs to the stranger's bedroom. The door was open so Mr Hall went straight in.

It was dark in the room, but Mr Hall thought he saw something very strange. There was a man's arm without a hand at the end. Then he was pushed out of the room and the door was locked behind him. He stood outside the door for a moment, trying to understand what he had seen. Then he went back outside.

'Is he all right?' asked the carter.

Mr Hall could not speak for a minute. He wanted to describe what he had seen in the bedroom, but he did not know how. 'Yes,' he said. 'He doesn't need any help. Let's get these boxes inside quickly.'

A few minutes later the stranger came back outside, wearing new trousers and gloves.

'I'm sorry, sir,' said the carter. 'Are you all right?'

'I'm fine,' said the stranger, angrily. 'It didn't break the skin. Now please can I have my things.'

As soon as the boxes were in the lounge the stranger opened them and began to take bottles out. There were hundreds. Small, fat, red bottles, small, thin bottles with a white liquid inside, blue bottles with 'poison[28]' written on them, large, green bottles, large, white bottles, small, yellow bottles, heavy brown bottles. The stranger opened box after box, and put the bottles carefully on the shelves, on the tables, on the desk, on the floor. Then he sat down at the desk under the window and started to work.

He was so busy with his writing and his bottles that when Mrs Hall brought in his lunch he did not hear her. She put the plate down on the table noisily and he half turned his head. He was not wearing his glasses, and it seemed to her that his eyes were very big. Then he put his glasses on.

'Please knock before you come in,' he said.

'I did knock, sir, but perhaps you didn't hear. You can lock the door if you prefer,' said Mrs Hall.

'A good idea,' he said.

'And, sir, all these bottles,' said Mrs Hall. 'How can I clean the room? Can I—'

'No! Don't touch them,' answered the stranger. 'If it's a problem, I can pay. Is a shilling²⁹ enough?'

'A shilling! Certainly, sir,' said Mrs Hall.

———

He worked all afternoon with the door locked. Most of the time the room was quiet. Once Mrs Hall heard a noise; a bottle broke, and then the stranger walked quickly around the room. She put her ear to the door. He was talking to himself: 'I can't go on,' he said. 'I need years, years. It's impossible!'

At five o'clock Mrs Hall took in his tea. There was broken glass in the corner of the room and a blue liquid on the floor.

'I know, I know,' said the stranger, angrily. 'Put it on my bill. If I break anything just put it on my bill.'

———

The stranger arrived in early February and for a few weeks there were no real problems. Mrs Hall talked to him several times about cleaning and noise. 'Put it on my bill,' said the stranger every time. He paid his bill every week and that was enough for Mrs Hall. Mr Hall did not like him, but he just stayed away.

The stranger spent most days working in the lounge. Some days he came down early and worked without a break until the evening. Other days he got up late, walked around the room talking to himself, sat by the fire and went to bed early. Nobody visited him. He received no letters, and he did not write any. He got angry quickly. And although Mrs Hall listened carefully outside the door when he was talking to himself, she understood nothing.

He did not often go out during the day. He preferred to go out in the early evening, and he was always very well covered. He frightened all the children that he met, and some adults, too, especially in the dark.

The people in the village did not agree about the stranger. Mrs Hall seemed to like him. Or perhaps she just liked his money. She told people that he was a scientist, and that he was doing important research. He had had an accident, she explained, so his hands and face were a strange colour, and he did not want people to see them.

Others in the village had different ideas. Some people thought he was on the run[P] from the police. They read the newspapers carefully, looking for news of a serious crime, but there was nothing. Others just thought that the man was mad. In general the stranger was not popular. People moved away when he walked through the village.

The local doctor, Dr Cuss, really wanted to find out more about the stranger. During May, he finally found a reason to visit him. He wanted to bring a nurse to live and work in the village, and he was going around asking everyone for money to pay her. He talked to Mrs Hall for a minute, and then knocked on the lounge door. 'Excuse me!' he said, and entered the room, closing the door behind him.

Mrs Hall was listening carefully to the two men talking. Then, after about ten minutes she heard a sudden shout of surprise. She heard the stranger laugh, then a chair fell over. The door opened and Dr Cuss came out of the lounge and ran outside. He went straight up the street, past the church, to the vicar[30]'s house.

'Mr Bunting!' he shouted to the vicar. 'Am I mad?' His eyes were wide and excited.

'What's happened?' asked the vicar.

'I went to see the stranger at the Coach and Horses. I wanted to ask him for some money for the village nurse. I went into the guests' lounge and I asked him about his research. "Is it slow?" I asked. "Yes," he answered. And then suddenly he told me his story. Somebody told him how to make a very special liquid. There were five different things in it and he had it all written on a piece of paper. In January he had everything he needed and he started to make the liquid. He put the paper down. The window was open, and the wind picked up the paper. It fell into the fire.'

Dr Cuss continued, looking hard at the vicar. 'I didn't really understand what the man was saying, and he saw it. So then, in the guests' lounge, the stranger lifted up his arm, and took off his glove. There was nothing there. Nothing! Then suddenly I felt a hand on my nose, pulling it. But there was nothing to see. I hit out and I felt an arm, but I couldn't see it. Then I ran!'

Mr Bunting looked at Dr Cuss. 'Interesting,' he said. 'Very interesting. A very strange story.'

3

The Burglary[31] *at the Buntings*

It was early one Monday morning and the vicar, Mr Bunting, and his wife were asleep in their house. Mrs Bunting woke up suddenly; she heard the bedroom door open and close. She listened, and heard the sound of feet walking out of the room and going down the stairs. She woke her husband. They both listened for a moment and then he got out of bed, picked up a heavy poker[32], and followed the sounds. He heard somebody downstairs trying to open his desk in the study[33] and then there was a loud sneeze[34].

'There was nothing there.'

It was very early in the morning and there was just a little light in the sky. The vicar walked quietly through the house with his poker in his hand. His wife followed him. There was a loud noise in the study, and the desk doors flew open. Then a match lit, and there was a sudden yellow light. Through the door Mr Bunting could see a lamp burning, and the desk with its doors wide open. But he could not see a burglar. He stood still for a moment.

Then he heard the sound of money. The burglar had found his money; he had two pounds and ten shillings in his desk! Now the vicar was angry. He ran into the room with his poker ready. Mrs Bunting ran in after him.

'Stop, now!' he shouted. The room was empty. Mr and Mrs Bunting looked all around the room, behind the curtains, and even under the desk.

'Who lit the lamp?' asked Mr Bunting.

'And where's our money? It's gone!' cried his wife.

There was a sudden sneeze just outside the door. They ran towards it. The kitchen door opened and closed. They ran into the kitchen. The door into the garden opened and closed, and they were alone in the house.

———

At about the same time on Monday morning, Mr Hall was also awake. The door of the stranger's bedroom was open, and Mr Hall went downstairs and saw that the front door was not locked. He went back up to the bedroom and looked inside. It was empty. He called his wife. As she came out of their room, somebody sneezed. They went into the bedroom.

She put her hand in the bed. 'It's cold,' she said. 'And look! His clothes are still there, on that chair. There's his hat!'

Suddenly the blankets[35] on the bed started to move. Something took hold of them in the centre, picked them up and threw them over the end of the bed. Then, suddenly, the stranger's hat flew up, around in a circle, and into Mrs Hall's face. Then a chair jumped up, laughed (with a laugh very like the stranger's), and started to chase[36] her. She ran out of the room, and her husband followed her. The door closed loudly and they heard the key turn.

A few minutes later they heard the door open again. The stranger came quickly down the stairs from his bedroom, into the guests' lounge. Mr Hall knocked on the door and opened it.

'Excuse me—' he began.

'Go away,' shouted the stranger. 'And close that door behind you.'

———

The stranger had gone down to the lounge at about half-past five in the morning. He rang three times for food, but Mrs Hall did not answer. Listening at the door, she could hear the noise of the glass bottles and the stranger talking to himself.

At twelve o'clock he opened the door, and called out in an angry voice, 'Mrs Hall!'

'Yes, sir,' she answered. 'Do you want your bill?'

'Where's my breakfast? Do you think I can live without food?' asked the stranger. He was shouting now.

'You haven't paid your bill,' she answered. 'I've been waiting for five days.'

'I told you on Saturday,' said the stranger. 'I'm waiting for some money to come to me. And it's arrived.'

'Has it?' asked Mrs Hall. 'And where did you get this money? You haven't had any letters. I have quite a lot of questions to ask you. First—'

The stranger raised his hands in the air. 'Stop!' he shouted. 'You don't understand who I am. I'll have to show you.'

Mr Hall and one or two other people were now standing behind Mrs Hall. Suddenly the stranger moved forwards and gave something to her. She took it and then she cried out and let go; a pink nose fell to the ground. Then the stranger removed[37] his hat and his bandages, his hair and his beard.

And there was nothing. They could see his clothes from the neck down, but, from the neck up, there was nothing.

Mr and Mrs Hall could not move for a moment. They stood with their mouths and eyes wide open. Then they turned and ran out into the street. Two minutes later, Mr Hall returned with Bobby Jaffers, the village policeman.

'Head or no head,' said Jaffers. 'I must arrest[38] him.' He was ready with his handcuffs.

Jaffers and Mr Hall went into the Coach and Horses. A man without a head was in the kitchen, holding some bread and a piece of cheese.

'That's him,' said Mr Hall.

'Sir!' said Jaffers. 'I must arrest you.'

The stranger picked up a knife. Jaffers took him by the arm, and, with his other hand, tried to catch the stranger's invisible neck. The stranger kicked out at Jaffers' legs, but Jaffers did not let go. Hall took the knife and threw it to the floor.

'Get his feet!' shouted the policeman, and Mr Hall tried to hold them. Suddenly the stranger stopped moving.

'All right,' he said. 'I won't fight you. I've done nothing wrong. I'm all here, but I'm invisible. I don't like it, but I am. But it's not a crime to be invisible.'

'No, it's not,' said Jaffers. 'That's not the crime. I'm looking for a burglar. You must come with me.'

'I'll come with you,' said the stranger. 'But no handcuffs.'

Then suddenly the stranger sat down, and started to take his clothes off.

'Stop him!' shouted Jaffers. 'If he takes all his clothes off …'

But he was too late. The clothes were on the floor and, somewhere in the room was the invisible stranger. Jaffers found him, and held him. But the stranger was fighting wildly, and it is very difficult to fight an Invisible Man. In a moment the stranger was out of the door, and Jaffers was lying on the kitchen floor.

4

Mr Thomas Marvel

Mr Thomas Marvel was not a man of fashion. His clothes were old, and the wind blew through the holes. He was not a thin man, and his beard was grey. He was sitting by the road about two-and-a-half miles[39] outside Iping. He wore no shoes, and his socks were full of holes. In front of him were two pairs of boots. There were his old boots, which were very old, and some newer boots. These newer boots were good boots, it was true, thought Mr Marvel. But they were much too big. So he sat and looked at the four boots and tried to make a decision. It was not an easy one.

'They're not very beautiful boots, are they?' said a Voice behind him.

'No,' said Mr Marvel. 'I've had better boots, and I've had worse. Usually I can find good boots in this part of the country, but not now. Nobody wants to give me good boots.'

'They're terrible people around here,' said the Voice.

'Terrible,' agreed Mr Marvel. He turned his head. No one was there, so he turned to the left. Nothing. He turned to the right. Nothing.

'Where are you?' asked Mr Marvel. He stood up.

'Don't be frightened,' said the Voice.

'But where are you?' asked Mr Marvel. 'Either I'm mad, or it's a dream.'

'You're not mad, and I'm not a dream,' said the Voice. And something pushed Mr Marvel hard in the stomach. 'Now, am I a dream?'

'All right,' said Mr Marvel. 'You're not a dream. But what are you?'

'It's simple,' said the Voice. 'I'm an Invisible Man.'

'I know that,' said Mr Marvel. 'But where are you hiding? How do you do it?'

'I'm not hiding anywhere[40],' said the Voice. 'I'm invisible. Don't you understand?'

'If you're invisible,' said Mr Marvel, 'give me your hand.'

He put his own hand out towards the Voice. An invisible hand took it. Mr Marvel felt the hand, and then the arm, and then the body. 'It's true,' he said. 'You really are invisible.'

He looked closely at where the Invisible Man was standing. 'Have you been eating bread and cheese?' he asked.

'Yes,' said the Invisible Man. 'You can sometimes see food for an hour or two after I eat it.'

'Well, that's something really wonderful,' said Mr Marvel. 'An Invisible Man!'

'It's not always wonderful,' said the Invisible Man. 'I need help. I need clothes. I need somewhere to hide, and other things. And you're going to help me.' He pushed Mr Marvel hard in the stomach. 'You must help me. Because if you don't help me …'

He pushed Mr Marvel again.

'All right,' said Mr Marvel. 'I'll help you.'

———

After a very exciting morning at the Coach and Horses, Iping was quiet again. The weather was good, and most people were outside. It was four o'clock, and in the guests' lounge, Dr Cuss and Mr Bunting were looking through the Invisible Man's books and bottles.

'Look at this,' said Dr Cuss, holding up three books. 'They're his diaries.'

He opened the first book. It was full of writing, but it was impossible to read. 'What is it?' he asked. 'Is it a code[41]?'

The two men looked through the pages carefully. They could not understand anything. Suddenly the door opened and Mr Marvel came in.

'This room's private,' said Mr Bunting. 'Please leave and shut that door behind you.'

Mr Marvel went out of the room, but he closed the door very slowly. Dr Cuss locked it behind him. The two men turned back to the diary, but only for a minute. Each men felt a hand on the back of his neck, pushing him down onto the table.

'What are you doing in my private room?' asked a Voice. 'And where are my clothes?'

The invisible hands moved away from the two necks.

'Don't move, now!' said the Voice. 'I've got a poker here.' The poker moved through the air and touched the nose of each man.

'Now,' said the Invisible Man. 'I need some clothes.' The poker touched Dr Cuss again. 'Take off your jacket, shirt and trousers.'

Dr Cuss had no choice. He took off his clothes. The Invisible Man picked up a tablecloth[42] and put the clothes inside it. Then he took his diaries. The Invisible Man opened the window and gave the diaries and the clothes to Mr Marvel, who was waiting for him outside. Then he climbed out of the window himself.

'Stop!' shouted Mr Bunting.

Mr Marvel did not stop. He started to run through the village holding the diaries and the tablecloth. Mr Hall climbed out of the window and started to run after him.

'Stop!' shouted Mr Hall. But then suddenly something invisible caught his leg. He flew several feet[43] through the air and fell heavily to the ground.

The Invisible Man was now very angry. He turned back and broke every window in the Coach and Horses, and he hit anybody who tried to come near him. Then he left the village of Iping for the last time.

5

Mr Marvel Tries to Escape

Later that same evening, Mr Marvel was walking along a road several miles from Iping. He was still carrying the diaries and the tablecloth. But he was not alone.

'If you try to run away again, I'll kill you,' said the Invisible Man. He was holding Mr Marvel's arm tightly[44].

'I didn't try to run away,' said Mr Marvel. 'I was lost.'

'And now. What am I to do now?' asked the Invisible Man. 'They all know about me. It will be in the newspapers tomorrow.'

'I can't help you anymore.' said Mr Marvel. 'I'm an old man. I'm ill. I can't walk far.'

'You'll have to help me,' said the Invisible Man. 'I've got no choice. You've got no choice.'

The two men walked on, into the night.

The next morning, Mr Marvel, with the diaries, but without the tablecloth, was sitting on a bench[45] by the road into Port Stowe. He looked very nervous. After about an hour, an old man with a newspaper came and sat down on the bench next to him.

'It's a nice day,' said the old man.

'Yes, it is,' answered Mr Marvel.

'You've got some books, I see,' said the old man. 'Wonderful things, books. You can read some very strange things in books.'

'Yes,' said Mr Marvel.

'And in newspapers,' continued the old man. 'You can read some wonderful things in newspapers, too.' He looked at Mr Marvel very closely. 'There's a strange story in this newspaper about an Invisible Man.'

'Is there?' asked Mr Marvel. 'Where is he? Is he somewhere in America or Australia?'

'No,' said the old man. 'Near here. In Iping. A lot of people have seen him. He hit a policeman and nearly killed him.'

Mr Marvel put his hand in his pocket and felt the money in there. His pocket was full of money.

'Does it say,' asked Mr Marvel slowly, 'if he had any friends?'

'No, it doesn't,' said the old man.

Mr Marvel looked at the old man. 'I've just been in Iping,' he said. 'I can tell you that it's not true.'

'Not true!' said the old man angrily. 'Of course it's true. It's in the newspaper. It must be true.'

'I know more about this Invisible Man than the newspaper,' said Mr Marvel. He was talking very quietly now, into the old man's ear.

'Do you?' asked the old man.

'Yes, you see –' Suddenly Mr Marvel stood up. His face went red. Something was pulling his ear.

'I must go,' he said.

'But what about the Invisible Man?' asked the old man. 'What do you know about him?'

'It's a lie[46],' said a Voice that did not sound quite like Mr Marvel's voice.

'But it's in the newspaper,' said the old man.

'Come on!' said the Voice. And Mr Marvel started to walk quickly down the road.

The old man sat on the bench and thought. Soon another man came along the road. He had another story. 'You won't believe this,' he told the old man. 'I was walking along the road there, and some money flew past me. I tried to catch it and something hit me. Hard.'

The old man did not believe that story. But it was true. Money was flying out of shops all around Port Stowe. And all that money was now going into Mr Marvel's pockets.

6

Dr Kemp at Home

One evening, Dr Kemp was working at home in his study. His house was on a hill above Port Burdock, and his study was on the top floor. The room had three windows, to the north, west and south, and he could see a long way from them. The study was full of scientific books and magazines. Under the north window was a microscope[47] and Dr Kemp was looking carefully into it, writing notes in a book next to him. Dr Kemp was a tall, thin man of about thirty, with fair hair. He was writing a book about his research. One day, he was sure, his research was going to be famous all over the world.

He stopped writing for a moment, and looked out of the window. Running along the road towards Port Burdock was a man with old boots and a beard.

'I expect that's another man with a stupid story about an Invisible Man,' said Dr Kemp to himself. 'Why do people believe it?' He turned back to his work.

People in the street could see the man more easily. They saw that Mr Marvel was very, very frightened and he was running as fast as possible. As he ran they could hear the sound of the money in his pockets.

Then something very strange happened. Up the hill, behind Mr Marvel, a dog suddenly turned and ran away from the road. Something was running down the hill. People could hear the feet on the ground, they could hear somebody breathing[48]. But they could see nothing.

'The Invisible Man!' somebody shouted. 'The Invisible Man is coming!'

The Jolly Cricketers is a friendly pub and hotel at the bottom of the hill on the edge of Port Burdock. A taxi driver, a large American with a black beard, and a policeman were inside, eating their lunch.

'What's that shouting?' asked the taxi driver. He stood up and looked out of the window.

'Perhaps there's a fire somewhere,' said the policeman.

The door flew open and Mr Marvel ran in. 'He's coming!' he shouted. 'The Invisible Man is coming. Help!'

The policeman stood up and locked the doors.

'Now,' said the American. 'You're safe. What's happening?'

Suddenly there was a loud knock at the door.

'Who's that?' asked the policeman.

'He'll kill me!' shouted Mr Marvel. 'He's got a knife. Please don't open the door. Where can I hide?'

The window broke with a loud noise.

'This Invisible Man,' said the American. 'Do we want to see him?'

Nobody answered.

'Let's unlock the door,' said the American. 'If he comes in …' He took his hand out of his pocket and showed them a gun.

'You can't do that,' said the policeman. 'That's murder[49]!'

'I know I'm not at home in the USA, so I can't kill him,' said the American. 'But in England I can fire[50] at his legs.' He went to the door, his gun in his hand, and unlocked it.

The door did not open.

'Are all the other doors locked?' asked Mr Marvel. 'Perhaps he's looking for another one.'

'Oh, no,' said the policeman. 'There's a back door into the kitchen.' He ran out of the room, into the kitchen. In a second he was back. He had a big kitchen knife in his hand.

'The back door was open,' said the policeman, 'But he's not in the kitchen. There are two women cooking in there and they didn't hear anything.'

Suddenly the door from the kitchen opened and in a second Mr Marvel was on the floor. There was a lot of shouting. The

'Let's unlock the door.'

American fired his gun across the room and broke a mirror. Then something pulled Mr Marvel into the kitchen and towards the back door. He held onto the back door. The Invisible Man was pulling him outside, but Mr Marvel did not want to go!

The taxi driver reached around Mr Marvel and found the Invisible Man's arm. 'I've got him,' he shouted.

The policeman came to help him, reaching around the other side of Mr Marvel. 'Yes. I've got him, too,' he said.

Mr Marvel was down on the floor. He tried to go under the legs of the two men and get back into the kitchen.

Now the Invisible Man was very angry. He hit the policeman and he kicked the taxi driver in the stomach. The taxi driver fell to the floor, and the Invisible Man was gone.

'Where is he?' asked the policeman, looking out of the door.

'I know what to do,' said the American. He took out his gun and fired, five times, into the garden. 'That's got him. Let's go and find the body.'

7

Dr Kemp's Visitor

Dr Kemp was still writing in his study when he heard the gun. 'What's that?' he said to himself. 'They're firing guns down in Port Burdock now. What's happening?'

It was dark now but there were lights in the street. He went to the south window and looked out. There were a lot of people outside the Jolly Cricketers. He watched them for a moment, and then went back to his desk. He had important work to do.

About an hour later, he heard the doorbell. He heard his servant[51] open the door. He waited for her to come upstairs, but she did not. He went to the door of his study and opened it. 'Who was that?' he called out to his servant.

'Nobody,' she answered. 'It was probably some children.'

Dr Kemp worked very late that night. He finished at about two o'clock in the morning, and went downstairs to get a drink before he went to bed. Walking back up to his bedroom he looked down and saw something red on the stairs. He reached down and touched it. It was blood.

He continued up the stairs to his bedroom. There was more blood on the door. He looked down at his hands. There was no cut in *his* skin.

He went into the room. There was blood on the blankets. Then he heard a Voice. 'Kemp,' it said, very quietly.

Dr Kemp was a man of science. He did not believe in invisible people. Then, coming towards him across the room, he saw a bandage. The bandage had blood on it and it went around … nothing.

'Kemp,' said the Voice again.

'What?' asked Dr Kemp.

'Kemp,' said the Voice. 'Don't be frightened. I'm an Invisible Man.'

Dr Kemp was not frightened. 'I thought it wasn't true,' he said. 'And you're wearing a bandage?'

'Yes,' said the Invisible Man.

Dr Kemp slowly put his hand out and touched the Invisible Man's hand.

'This is all a story,' he said. 'It can't be true.'

'Kemp,' said the Invisible Man, 'I need your help.'

He caught Dr Kemp's arm and held it tightly. Dr Kemp tried to get away, but the Invisible Man pushed him down onto the bed. Dr Kemp opened his mouth to shout, and the Invisible Man pushed some of the blanket between his teeth.

'Listen to me,' said the Invisible Man.

Dr Kemp stopped moving.

'I'm going to take the blanket out of your mouth,' said the Invisible Man. 'But if you shout, I'll hit you. I am an Invisible Man, and I need your help. Do you remember me, Kemp? My name's Griffin.'

He took the blanket away.

'We were students together,' said the Invisible Man. 'You remember me. I've got very fair hair.'

'I don't understand,' said Dr Kemp. 'Where's Griffin?'

'I'm here. I'm Griffin,' said the Invisible Man.

'But how?' asked Dr Kemp. 'How are you invisible?'

'I did an experiment,' said the Invisible Man. 'Just a normal science experiment. I worked for years on research into light. And finally I found out how to become invisible. It's easier for me than for some people because my hair is white – I'm an albino[52]. I've done it, but now I need help because I can't go back. And I need some food and drink.'

The Invisible Man picked up Dr Kemp's drink and finished it. 'Can you give me some clothes?' he asked.

Dr Kemp went to a cupboard and took out some trousers and a shirt.

'Some shoes, too,' said the Invisible Man. 'And some food.'

Dr Kemp gave him the clothes and shoes and then went downstairs to find some food. He came back with some bread and cold meat and put them on a table in front of his guest. The Invisible Man started to eat.

'Well.' said Dr Kemp. 'This is strange. Is your arm all right?'

'Yes,' said the Invisible Man.

'What about the gun I heard?' asked Dr Kemp. 'What was that?'

'There was a man.' said the Invisible Man. 'He was helping me. He took my money.'

'Is he invisible too?' asked Dr Kemp.

'No,' answered the Invisible Man.

'Did you fire the gun?' asked Kemp.

'No,' said the Invisible Man. 'I don't know who it was. They were all stupid and frightened. I'm still hungry, Kemp. Get me some more food.'

Dr Kemp went downstairs and came back with more food. The Invisible Man finished the food. Dr Kemp watched the food disappear. It was very strange.

'How did you do it?' he asked. 'It's wonderful!'

'Let me rest for a few minutes,' said the Invisible Man. 'I'll tell you later.'

But he did not. His arm was hurting badly and he was getting ill. He started talking about Mr Marvel.

'He's got my money,' he said. 'Why didn't I kill him?'

'Where did you get the money?' asked Dr Kemp.

'I can't tell you tonight,' said the Invisible Man. 'I must sleep. I haven't slept for three days.'

'You can sleep here,' said Dr Kemp. 'But why haven't you slept before?'

'Because I don't want to be caught.' said the Invisible Man.

The look on Dr Kemp's face changed suddenly.

'Oh no,' said the Invisible Man, watching him. 'Now you want to catch me!'

'I don't,' promised Dr Kemp. 'You're safe with me. You can sleep here, in my room.'

The Invisible Man checked the room very carefully. He opened and closed the windows, and he checked all the locks. Finally he relaxed. 'I'll tell you everything tomorrow, Kemp,' he said. 'But I must sleep now. Good night.'

'Good night,' said Dr Kemp, leaving his bedroom. He heard the door lock behind him.

He went downstairs to his sitting room. 'Invisible!' he said to himself. 'Is it possible? Are there any invisible animals? Yes, in the sea and in rivers. There are a lot of them, so it's possible in water. But is it possible in the air? Even if a man was made of glass, you could see him.'

He picked up a newspaper. He read about the strange things in Iping. Jaffers nearly dead. Dr Cuss and Mr Hall. The poker. The broken windows.

'He's invisible, but he's mad, too,' he thought.

Dr Kemp did not sleep that night. Morning came quickly, and he waited for the day's newspaper to arrive. It had the same story about Iping and Port Stowe. But now there was also a story about Port Burdock and the Jolly Cricketers.

'He's invisible,' he thought. 'So he can do anything to anyone. What do I do?'

He sat down at his desk and wrote a short letter. On the envelope he wrote: *Colonel Adye, Port Burdock Police.*

Then he heard the Invisible Man upstairs in his bedroom. He was awake. He heard his feet, and then a shout. The Invisible Man was very angry. Dr Kemp ran upstairs and knocked on the bedroom door.

8

The Invisible Man in London

'Are you all right?' asked Dr Kemp, when the Invisible Man opened the bedroom door.

'It's this arm,' said the Invisible Man. 'It still hurts.'

'Everybody knows about you,' said Dr Kemp. 'They know about Iping and Port Stowe, and Port Burdock. It's in all the newspapers. But nobody knows where you are now. There's breakfast upstairs.'

They went upstairs to Kemp's study. Dr Kemp watched the Invisible Man eat. He was wearing a shirt and trousers, but of course Dr Kemp could not see his hands and head.

'Tell me,' said Dr Kemp. 'How did you do it?'

'It isn't simple,' said the Invisible Man. 'It's all in my diaries. I haven't got them now. Marvel's got them. But it's all there.' He stopped for a moment and then started again. 'Listen, Kemp. Think about light. When light reaches something, it goes into it, or it comes back from it. You only see something when you see the light from it. If you don't see the light, it's invisible. Do you understand?'

'Yes,' said Dr Kemp. 'I understand that.'

'Now,' continued The Invisible Man. 'Glass is not invisible, you can see it. But when you put glass in water it is invisible.'

'Yes,' said Dr Kemp.

'But a person is much better than glass, because a person is mostly water,' said the Invisible Man. 'So it's not a big change. The biggest problems are the blood and the hair. For me, the hair wasn't a problem – my hair is almost white. But the blood was a big problem. I knew what to do about the blood, but I needed money. I took the money from my father. But it wasn't his money, and he killed himself.'

The Invisible Man was standing by the window, looking out.

'You're tired,' said Dr Kemp. 'Come and sit down.'

The Invisible Man sat down. Dr Kemp stood between him and the window.

'Last year I had a room in an old house in London – in Great Portland Street,' continued the Invisible Man. 'I had everything I needed there. I started to do experiments. I'll tell you exactly what I did one day, Kemp, but I have to get my diaries back first. I began with a piece of white wool. It was wonderful to watch. It became invisible quite quickly, but then I could put out my hand and touch it. Then I heard a white cat outside the window. I opened it, and the cat came in. It was hungry and I gave it some milk. I gave it some very special drugs[53] to take the colour out of its blood and hair. Then I put it to sleep and did the experiment.'

35

'Then I put it to sleep and did the experiment.'

'Did it work?' asked Dr Kemp.

'Almost,' said the Invisible Man. 'The back of its eyes didn't change colour. You could see nothing of the cat except the eyes.'

'Strange,' said Dr Kemp.

'Yes,' said the Invisible Man. 'I don't know why the eyes didn't change.'

'How long did it take?' asked Dr Kemp.

'Three or four hours,' said the Invisible Man. 'The hair took a long time, and, as I said, the back of the eyes didn't change at all. I was tired at the end of it. The cat was still asleep, and I went to sleep as well. In the middle of the night the cat woke up and it woke me up. It was walking around the room. I turned the light on, and of course, I could only see its green eyes. I opened the window and it went out.'

'So there's an invisible cat, too,' said Dr Kemp.

'If it's still alive,' said the Invisible Man. 'It's probably dead now. It was alive a few days later, I know that. There was a crowd of people in the street looking for a cat. They could hear it, but they couldn't see it.'

The Invisible Man stopped. He did not saying anything for a minute or two.

'I remember the day that I became invisible very well,' he continued. 'It was a beautiful, cold, sunny day in January. I went for a walk in the park. I knew that I had to work quickly because I had no more money. I went back to my room and had lunch, and then went to sleep.

'I woke up after about an hour,' continued the Invisible Man. 'Someone was knocking on the door. It was my landlord. He was worried. What was I doing in the room? Why all the noise? What was that cat noise? He came into the room and started looking at things. I told him to go. He refused. In the end I pushed him out of the door and locked it. He shouted at me from outside the door, but I didn't listen.

37

'But this worried me,' he continued. 'I knew that I didn't have very much time. I couldn't move to another room because I didn't have enough money. There was only one way to escape – invisibility. It was the answer to all my problems. But first I needed to find somewhere for my diaries. There's a shop in Great Portland Street where you can send letters and they look after them for you. It's not cheap, but it seemed the best answer. I found a box, put my diaries in it, took it to the Post Office and posted them. I was ready.'

'So what did you do next?' asked Dr Kemp.

'I went back to my room,' answered the Invisible Man. 'The first thing I needed was the drugs to take the colour out of my blood. I drank them and sat down and waited. After a few minutes there was a knock at the door. It was the landlord again. He wanted me to leave the house immediately. But when he saw me he looked very frightened and ran off back down the stairs. I shut the door, and locked it, and looked in the mirror. I looked awful. My face was completely white, like a white stone.

'It was a long night,' continued the Invisible Man. 'My body hurt all over, and I thought for some time that I was dying. But in the early morning I looked at my hands. They were almost invisible. After another hour or two I was completely invisible.'

'How did you feel?' asked Dr Kemp.

'At the end I felt fine, but I was so tired,' answered the Invisible Man. 'I went to sleep and slept until about twelve o'clock. Then I woke up, hearing voices outside my door. It was the landlord. I talked to him but I didn't open the door. He had his two sons with him, young men of twenty-three or twenty-four. They started to break down the door, so I didn't have much time. I opened the window, climbed out, and closed it again. My room was high up, and I couldn't climb down to the ground. But I waited outside and looked back into my room. Just at that moment the door fell into the room and the three men followed it.

'They were very surprised to find the room empty,' he continued. 'One of the young men came to the widow, opened it and looked out. His eyes were a foot from my face, but he couldn't see me. He went back into the room and the three men talked for a few minutes. I wasn't worried about these three men; they weren't scientists. But I didn't want a scientist to see my room. There was too much information about my experiment. I climbed back into the room and carefully walked past the three men, out of the door, and down the stairs. I waited until the room was empty again. Then I went back upstairs, found some papers, and lit a fire.'

'You burnt your room?' asked Dr Kemp. 'But someone could have been hurt.'

'I had no choice,' said the Invisible Man. 'Then I left the house quietly and went into the street. I had wonderful plans.'

'My first difficulty was going downstairs,' he continued. 'It's difficult to walk downstairs when you can't see your feet. It was a little difficult to open the door, because I couldn't see my hand. But in the street, at first, it was a little easier. I was excited. I wanted to surprise people, to make them jump^P, to take their hats and throw them in the air.

'Then suddenly I was knocked to the ground,' said the Invisible Man. 'A man with a heavy wooden box – it was full of bottles – walked into me. This really hurt me, but the man looked so surprised that I laughed. He looked more surprised when I took the box away from him. Then another man tried to take the box. He couldn't see me, but he hit me. The box fell to the ground, and suddenly there was a crowd around me. I had to push my way out.

'I walked down into Oxford Street, but it was no good,' he continued. 'People couldn't see me. They walked into me and pushed me. And I was cold. It was January and I had no clothes. I had no shoes and there was ice in the street. Then I saw a taxi in the street next to me and I quietly climbed in. The driver didn't hear me, and for a few minutes I was safe. The taxi went slowly along Oxford Street and I thought about my future. Ten minutes before, I had been very excited about a future as an Invisible Man. Now it was very different. I really didn't know what to do.

'A tall woman with five or six yellow books shouted to my taxi. I jumped out just in time,' the Invisible Man went on. 'I started to run quickly, and I was crying as I did. I was soon in quiet streets, but my problems continued. A small, white dog started to follow me. He couldn't see me, but he could smell me. He jumped up at my legs. I ran faster, but he still followed me. I turned a corner, and heard music. A great crowd of people were walking down the street towards me. A band was playing and people were singing loudly. I couldn't pass a crowd like that; they would walk all over me. I turned to one of the houses in the street, and ran up the steps⁵⁷ to the front door. I was out of the street and I hoped that nobody would come out of the door.

'Luckily,' continued the Invisible Man, 'the dog was very interested in the music and he stopped following me. Unluckily, two boys stopped in the street near the steps. "Look at this," said one of them to his friend. "Somebody with no shoes has walked up those steps." I looked at the steps and I could see where my wet feet had walked up. "You're right," said the other boy. "But he hasn't walked down again, has he? There's some blood on the steps, too. And look, there!" he looked down at my feet. He couldn't see my feet, but there was dirty water and blood on them. He could see that.

'The first boy looked at my feet,' the Invisible Man went on, 'And he put out his hand to touch them. A man stopped to watch, and then a girl. This was getting dangerous. I pushed past them and ran down the street, but they followed me

'And look, there!'

closely. "What's happening?" somebody asked. "There are feet running down the street," answered one of the boys.

'I soon had six or seven people following me,' he continued. 'I ran as fast as I could, turning right and left. I escaped, and then I stopped for a moment and tried to get my feet clean. I was not so cold now, after running. But now it was starting to snow, and I decided that it was time to go home. I walked back towards my room, but when I turned into the street, the house was burning brightly. I had lost everything, except my diaries.'

The Invisible Man stopped talking for a moment. Dr Kemp looked nervously out of the window. 'Yes?' he said. 'Go on.'

9

In the Department Store

So that is how my new, invisible, life began,' continued the Invisible Man. 'I had nowhere to go. It was snowing, and I was cold, tired and ill. I did not think that anybody would help me. I needed to get out of the cold, and I suddenly had a brilliant idea. I walked to Tottenham Court Road and went to Omniums, the department store. Do you know that shop? You can buy everything there – food, furniture, clothes, and lots of other useful things. The doors were not open, but I followed somebody in quite easily. At first, I was in the department where they sell gloves and hats. I walked through that, and went upstairs. There was a big section for beds and bedroom furniture. I found a corner there where I could hide and wait for the evening. I wanted to spend the night there, find some food and clothes, and perhaps sleep in one of the beds.

'At six o'clock the store started to close for the night. The last customers left, and a group of young shop assistants went through the store, organizing everything for the next day. Then a group of cleaners went through the whole store. I had to be careful, because they cleaned every corner of the building. Finally the cleaners left and I was alone.

'I started with the clothes. I found some trousers, a shirt, a jacket and a coat. I also found a big hat which covered a lot of my face. I began to feel human again. Upstairs there was a restaurant, and I got myself some cold food and made some coffee. Then I found some chocolate for dessert. I moved on to the toy department, where I saw some shiny, pink plastic noses. That gave me some useful ideas. I wanted some dark glasses as well. Omniums didn't sell glasses, but I knew that I could get them somewhere else. Finally I found a comfortable bed.

'Before I went to sleep, I thought about my plans for the morning. I planned to wear all my new clothes, and to cover my face with a handkerchief. I could take money from the store, and then go out and buy some dark glasses. Then I could be ready for my adventure.'

'Did you sleep well in the department store?' asked Dr Kemp, still looking out of the window.

'Very well,' said the Invisible Man. 'I woke in the early morning, and for a moment I didn't know where I was. Then I heard some people. Two men were talking, and walking through the store. I jumped out of bed and started to run. I was still wearing my new clothes so I wasn't invisible. "Who's that?" shouted one of the men. "Stop!" shouted the other. I went round a corner and ran into a boy of about fifteen. Remember, he could see my clothes, but I had no face! He shouted, and I pushed him and ran past. I found a sofa, and hid on the floor behind it. I was still wearing my clothes, because I wanted to keep them, but I knew that I had to take them off now. I pulled them off as quickly as I could.

'"This way, policeman!" somebody shouted. Three men and a policeman came round the corner. I was invisible now, and I

43

ran off. Of course, they found my clothes and started looking for me everywhere, but I was safe. I wanted to keep the clothes, but it was impossible. I stayed in the store for an hour or two more, and then left. I needed another plan.

'Do you understand now, Kemp, the problems that I had?' asked the Invisible Man. 'I had no clothes, and it was the middle of winter. And I couldn't eat. Did you know that when I eat the food is visible for about an hour?'

'I never thought of that,' said Dr Kemp.

'Neither did I,' said the Invisible Man. 'And snow, of course, was a problem, because when I walked in it you could see me. Even rain was a problem, because it didn't fall through me. It just ran off. And when I got dirty – and London is a very dirty city – it was easy to see me. I decided that I needed to get out of London. I was looking for a shop that I knew, and I was able to find it quickly. It was a shop which sold things for theatres; everything that an actor needs. It was an old shop in an old building, with a house above it. I pushed the door, and went in. Of course, the bell rang, but for a moment nobody came into the shop. My plan was clear to me. I wanted at first to hide upstairs. Then, when the shop was empty, I planned to find the glasses, nose and wig[55] that I needed, take some money, and leave.

'At last, the door at the back of the shop opened, and an old man came in. He looked around for his customer. He was angry when he saw that the shop was empty. "Those boys!" he shouted. He opened the front door and looked out into the street. He closed the door and kicked it. Then he turned to the back of the shop. I wanted to follow him into the house, but I made a noise, and he heard me. He ran through the back door into the house and closed it in my face. But he was worried. After a minute he opened the door again, and came back into the shop. He looked around the shop carefully, talking to himself. I went through the back door into his living room.

'The living room had cheap, simple furniture. The old man's breakfast was still on the table, and soon he came back and started to eat again. I was hungry again, and it was awful to see, and smell, the food.

There were three doors into the living room. One went into the shop, and it was now closed again. There were two other doors, also closed. I couldn't leave the room until he opened one of them.

'At last, he finished his breakfast and he picked up his plate and cup. He opened the door into the kitchen. He didn't close the door because his hands were full, so I followed him. But the old, stone floor was cold, so I went back into the living room and sat by the fire. The fire wasn't very big so, stupidly, I put some more wood on it. Of course the old man heard me and came back. He looked around the room for a minute or two, and then went back to the kitchen. He closed the door again. This man loved closing doors.

'I waited in the living room for a very long time. Finally he came back and opened the third door. I managed to follow him and I found myself on the stairs. We went up, but he stopped suddenly, and I almost hit him. He was listening very carefully. He went down the stairs again, past me, and then back up. Suddenly he shouted, "If there's anyone in this house …" He put his hand in his pocket, looking for something, but he didn't find it. Then he went downstairs again. I didn't follow him this time, but sat at the top of the stairs and waited. He came back up the stairs again and opened a door at the top. He went into a room, and closed the door behind him quickly.

'Now I could visit the rest of the house. It was very old and dirty. I found a room with a number of actors' masks[56]. I also found a room full of old clothes. They probably came from theatres, too. I started to look through the clothes, and of course the old man heard me. He came into the room quietly, and this time he was holding an old gun. I didn't move. "It's her," he said to himself. Then he went out of the room. He closed the door, and I heard the key turn.

'Now I was locked in. I didn't know what to do. I decided to look at the clothes again, and I reached up to a shelf on the wall. It fell down with a terrible noise, and the old man came back and looked around the room again. He was very frightened. I went out of the room, onto the stairs, and I think he heard me. He came out of the room and locked it. Then he took some keys out of his pocket and he started to go round the house locking every door. I was now very angry with him. I was sure that he was alone in the house, so I knocked him on the head.'

'Knocked him on the head?' asked Dr Kemp.

'Yes,' said the Invisible Man. 'I knocked him on the head with a chair. He fell down the stairs.'

'But you can't do that!' said Dr Kemp.

'Look, Kemp,' said the Invisible Man. 'I had no choice. I needed to get out of that house, and I needed the clothes. So I tied him up in a blanket.'

'A blanket!' said Dr Kemp.

'Yes,' said the Invisible Man. 'I made the blanket into a bag and put him in it.'

'But, the law!' said Dr Kemp.

'Oh,' answered the Invisible Man, angrily. 'There's no law for me! You think I'm a burglar, too. But I had no choice.'

'But what happened to the old man?' asked Dr Kemp. 'Was he all right?'

The Invisible Man was now very angry. 'I don't know,' he said. 'But, Kemp, you must understand. It wasn't my fault. I had no choice. And that old man. He was so stupid, with his gun and his keys.'

Dr Kemp wanted to say more, but he understood that the Invisible Man was now very dangerous. He decided to change the subject.

'So, what did you do next?' he asked.

'I was hungry,' said the Invisible Man, 'So I went downstairs and found some bread and cheese. Then I went back upstairs. I went past the old man – he didn't move – and went back to the room with the old clothes. I put on the clothes that I wanted, and then found a good mask, a beard and a wig. I was beginning to look like a normal man. I needed shoes and socks. I couldn't find any socks, but the old man's boots were all right. I took a bag, because I had things to carry. I needed money, and I spent a lot of time looking for it. I found about five pounds in the shop, and then another eight pounds in the old man's bedroom. I looked at myself in a mirror, again. I decided it was time to go outside.'

'Do you know what happened to the old man in the shop?' asked Dr Kemp.

'I don't know,' said the Invisible Man. 'And I don't want to know!'

'So where did you go next?' asked Dr Kemp.

'I was feeling happier,' said the Invisible Man. 'I knew that I could get money easily. If I wanted more, I could just take off my clothes and go into a shop. I decided to go to a good restaurant and then check into an excellent hotel. Life was going to be good. I went into a restaurant and ordered some lunch. I finished my order, and then remembered that I had a problem. It was not possible to eat with my mask on. And it wasn't possible to take my mask off. I left the restaurant immediately, both hungry and angry.

'I went to a different restaurant and asked for a private room. I told them that I had had an accident and didn't want to eat in public. Then I sat alone in that private room and thought about things. It was snowing outside now. When I was invisible it was possible for me to get a lot of things. But I couldn't enjoy them. There was no hope for me, certainly not in London.'

'So how did you get to Iping?' asked Dr Kemp. He wanted the Invisible Man to talk more.

'I went to Iping to work,' said the Invisible Man. 'I had had enough. It's been interesting but I don't want to be invisible any more. That's why I need your help. I want to show you some of my ideas.'

'Did you go straight to Iping?' asked Dr Kemp.

'Yes,' said the Invisible Man. 'I went to Great Portland Street and got my diaries. I ordered some of the things I needed for my experiments. Then I got the train to Iping. I wanted somewhere quiet to work. It went well for a few weeks. And then, the day before yesterday …'

'I read about it in the newspaper,' said Dr Kemp. 'There was a lot of fighting.'

'Yes,' said the Invisible Man. 'I was very angry. I worked for years, and then those stupid people stopped me from finishing. Did I kill that policeman?'

'No,' said Dr Kemp.

'Did I kill anybody?' asked the Invisible Man.

'Luckily you didn't,' said Dr Kemp.

'If anybody else gets in my way,' said the Invisible Man, 'I will kill them. I just get so angry!'

10

The Search for the Invisible Man

And now,' asked Dr Kemp, looking out of the window again, 'what are we going to do?' He moved in front of his guest. He did not want the Invisible Man to see the three men who were walking up the road. They were walking too slowly, Dr Kemp thought.

The Invisible Man did not answer.

'Why did you come to Port Burdock?' asked Dr Kemp. 'What was your plan?'

'It's near the sea,' said the Invisible Man. 'I wanted to find a ship and get out of the country. I planned to get to France, and then get on a train south. I thought perhaps to Spain, or even North Africa. I wanted to find somewhere with better weather, where I didn't need clothes. Then I could live an invisible life easily. But I needed my diaries and I don't know where they are. Marvel's got them, or he's hidden them somewhere. If I can find him, I'll ...'

'So you need to get your diaries first,' said Dr Kemp.

'But where is Marvel?' asked the Invisible Man. 'Do you know where he is?'

'Yes, I do. He's in the town police station,' said Dr Kemp. 'He asked them to lock him up.'

'The dirty dog!' cried the Invisible Man.

'It makes things a little difficult,' said Dr Kemp.

'Well, I must get the diaries,' said the Invisible Man. 'Without them, I will be invisible forever.'

'Yes, I understand,' said Dr Kemp. Could he hear people walking outside? Had they arrived? He must keep talking. But then the Invisible Man spoke.

'But finding your house like this,' he said, 'changes everything. This is my first piece of luck. You know me. You're a scientist, you understand. You can help me. Did you tell anyone else that I'm here?'

'I thought you wanted it to be a secret,' answered Dr Kemp.

'Yes,' said the Invisible Man. 'Good. My big mistake, Kemp, was to do the experiment alone. I need someone to work with me because I need somewhere to live and somewhere to eat. With that person – you – a thousand things are possible. I now understand, Kemp, what I can do best, and what I can't do. I can listen to people and take money, but it's not easy. But when

I'm invisible I can easily get close to people, and I can easily escape. So it's excellent for fighting and excellent for killing.'

Dr Kemp moved nervously. Was there somebody downstairs?

'Because,' said the Invisible Man, 'we must do some killing.'

'Why?' asked Dr Kemp.

'We need to kill a few people at the beginning,' said the Invisible Man. 'We need to frighten people. Then they will do what I want. I'll give orders, and if people don't listen, then I will have to kill them.'

'I see,' said Dr Kemp. But he wasn't listening to the Invisible Man. He was listening to his front door. It opened, and then closed again.

'But if I help you,' said Dr Kemp, 'the police will arrest me.'

'They won't know about you!' said the Invisible Man. 'What's that noise downstairs?'

'It's nothing,' said Dr Kemp. There *was* a noise, so he needed to speak loudly. 'I don't agree, Griffin. I don't think it's possible. It's one person, or two people, against the world. We need to get the world on your side[P]. Let's write something together and get it into the newspaper. Then other people will help us as well—'

The Invisible Man interrupted[57]. 'There's somebody coming up the stairs,' he said in a quiet voice.

'I don't think so,' said Dr Kemp.

'Let me see,' he answered and went to the door. Dr Kemp tried to stop him.

'You have told the police!' cried the Invisible Man. He immediately started to take off his clothes.

Now they could both hear feet on the stairs. Dr Kemp opened the door and jumped outside. He closed the door quickly. The key was in the door, ready, but it fell out on to the floor. The Invisible Man opened the door a few inches and the two men pushed and pulled at it for a minute. Then an invisible hand came through the door and caught Dr Kemp's neck. He had to take his hands away from the door. The door opened suddenly, Dr Kemp fell back onto the floor, and a shirt flew down on top of him.

On the stairs below him was Colonel Adye, the head of the Port Burdock police. He saw Dr Kemp fall, and then the shirt fly through the air. Then, suddenly, something heavy hit him, and then something kicked him. He was thrown down the stairs. He heard the two policeman downstairs shout, and then the front door opened and closed.

He sat up. Dr Kemp was coming down the stairs towards him. There was blood on Dr Kemp's face and he was holding some clothes.

'He's escaped!' said Dr Kemp. 'What do we do now?'

————

Dr Kemp tried to explain everything to Colonel Adye. At first, Adye found it all very hard to understand, but after a few moments things began to get a little clearer.

'He's quite mad,' said Dr Kemp, 'And he thinks only of himself. He's already hurt a lot of people, and he's broken the law in other ways. He will start to kill people soon, and nothing can stop him. He is now both mad and angry.'

'We must catch him,' said Adye. 'And we must do it as soon as possible.'

'But how?' asked Dr Kemp, and suddenly he was full of ideas. 'You must begin at once, and use every man that you've got. You must keep him near Port Burdock. If he gets away he could go anywhere. He says he'll kill people, and I believe him! You must watch all the trains, roads and ships. Ask the army to help you. There's only one thing that will keep him in Port Burdock – his diaries. There's a man in your police station, his name's Marvel ...'

'I know,' said Adye. 'The diaries, yes, he wants his diaries.'

'He needs to eat and sleep,' said Dr Kemp. 'You must stop him. Food must be locked up, and houses, too. If we're lucky there will be rain and the nights will be cold. Everyone must look for him. He's a serious danger to everyone, Adye, and you must catch him.'

'I must go back to the police station and start organizing,' said Adye. 'Can you come, too? We need your help. I'll talk to some people from the army and the railway.'

The two men went down the stairs quickly. The front door was open, and the two policemen were outside, looking around the garden. 'He's got away[58], sir,' said one.

'We must get back to the police station quickly,' said Adye. 'One of you, go and get us a taxi. Now, Kemp, what else do you think we can do?'

'Dogs,' said Dr Kemp. 'They can't see him, but they can smell him.'

'Good,' said Adye. 'They have dogs at the prison in Halstead. I'll talk to the people there. What else?'

'One thing,' said Dr Kemp. 'You can see the food after he's eaten. So he has to hide for an hour or two. You must have men looking everywhere, behind every tree, in every corner. And if he carries things, you can see them. So he can't carry anything for a long time. You need to lock up any knives and guns so he can't use them.'

'Good,' said Adye, writing it all down.

'On the roads.' said Dr Kemp, and then he stopped for a moment.

'Yes?' asked Adye.

'I don't like it, but you must do this. Put broken glass on the roads.' said Dr Kemp. 'Remember he has no shoes.'

'I don't know,' said Adye. 'I don't want to do that. But I'll get some glass ready. I hope we won't need it.'

'We must do everything we can,' said Dr Kemp. 'Everything!'

11

The Wicksteed Murder

The Invisible Man was now extremely angry. He ran out of Dr Kemp's house and out into the street. A boy was playing there, and the Invisible Man picked him up and threw him across the road. The fall broke the poor boy's foot. The Invisible Man then went up the hill and into the forest around Hintondean. He sat in the forest for most of the morning. He was thinking about his next plan. He was very angry with Dr Kemp. The meeting with Dr Kemp had given him hope. For an hour or two it seemed that he had a future. But now he knew that he was alone.

That morning he made a big mistake – he stayed near Port Burdock. He had the time, early that morning, to get far away. The police were not yet organized, and the town was not ready. Unluckily for him, but luckily for the rest of the country, he stayed in Hintondean.

During the morning, Dr Kemp and Colonel Adye worked quickly. Posters went up on walls all around the town. Trains were running, but their doors were locked. And in a circle of twenty miles around Port Burdock groups of men were getting ready with guns and heavy sticks. They closed the roads and were ready to walk through every inch[59] of countryside. Police on horses visited every house. Stay inside your houses, they told everyone, and lock your doors. They closed the schools and helped the children to get home safely.

In the early afternoon the Invisible Man started moving again. He left the Hintondean forest, and now he was carrying a heavy metal poker. Nobody knows where he found it.

Mr Wicksteed was a man of about forty-five who worked near Hintondean. The last person to see him alive, just after two o'clock, was a little girl. She saw him running across a field. He was waving his stick and hitting at something that was moving across the ground. He was probably trying to hit the Invisible Man's poker. Mr Wicksteed went behind some trees and the girl went home.

Mr Wicksteed did not know about the Invisible Man, but he did see the poker. He followed it into some trees and the Invisible Man found himself in a corner. He could not escape easily. But he did not need to kill Mr Wicksteed, and he certainly did not need to hit him fifteen or twenty times with a heavy, metal poker. The Invisible Man left the body and walked off through the fields. Late in the afternoon, two men near Fern Bottom heard somebody laughing and crying, and then shouting. Perhaps the Invisible Man really was mad.

The police found Mr Wicksteed's body late that afternoon. The poker, covered with blood, was on the ground. The Invisible Man had killed somebody for the first time.

It was a difficult afternoon for the Invisible Man. He read the posters about himself, and he found houses locked. He tried the railway stations, but it was impossible to travel. In the fields he saw men with guns and sticks. There were dogs, too. He was in a difficult corner and he did not know where to go, or what to do next. But he found some food somewhere and he slept a little in the trees. When morning came, he felt strong again and ready for a fight.

At one o'clock the following day, the postman brought a strange letter to Dr Kemp. It was written in pencil on an old and dirty piece of paper.

'You have been very busy and very clever,' it said. 'But you cannot win. You looked for me all day, but you didn't find me. I've found food, and I've slept. So now the real game is beginning. I am the king today in Port Burdock. This is the first day of a new year: The Year of the Invisible Man. I am

Invisible Man the First! And today one man will die. His name is Kemp. He can lock his house, he can hide, he can ask the police to watch him. But he will die. And anybody who helps him will die, too.'

Dr Kemp read the letter twice. 'That's him,' he thought. 'That's the Invisible Man. And he will do it, if he can.'

Dr Kemp left his lunch for a moment and went up to his study. He called his servant and told her to lock all the doors and windows in the house, and close the shutters[60]. Then he went to his bedroom and took a small gun out of a cupboard. He checked it carefully and put it in his pocket. Then he wrote a short letter to Colonel Adye and gave it to his servant. 'Take this to the police station,' he said. Then he went back to finish his lunch.

He ate slowly, thinking. Once he hit the table hard. 'If he wants to kill me he must come here. Then we can catch him!' he cried.

He went up to his study, closing every door behind him. There were no shutters up here at the top of the house; it was too high. He looked out of the window. 'It is a game,' he said to himself. 'But it's a game that I think we can win.'

He looked out at the hills. 'He needs food every day,' he thought. 'That's not going to be easy. Did he really sleep last night? I don't think so. Today the weather is good, but tomorrow it may rain. We need some cold weather.'

'Perhaps he's watching me now.' he thought.

Something hit the wall, just above the window. Dr Kemp jumped back. 'I'm getting nervous,' he said to himself. 'That was only a bird.' But he did not go back to the window for a few minutes.

Then he heard the bell ring. Somebody was at the front door. He ran downstairs and started to unlock it carefully. Then he heard Adye's voice, and opened the door a few inches.

'Somebody's attacked[61] your servant,' said Adye.

'What!' said Dr Kemp.

'He took the letter away from her,' said Adye. 'He's near here. Let me in!'

Dr Kemp opened the door a little and Adye came in. Then he closed and locked it again quickly.

'The Invisible Man took the letter out of her hand,' said Adye. 'It frightened her, but she isn't hurt. She's at the police station now. What did you say in the letter?'

'I'm so stupid,' said Dr Kemp. 'Look!' He took Adye into the sitting room and gave him the Invisible Man's letter. Adye read it and looked up in surprise.

'So he's coming here,' said Adye.

There was a loud noise of breaking glass. It came from upstairs.

'That's a window,' said Dr Kemp. They moved quickly, but a second window broke while they were on the stairs. In Dr Kemp's study, two of the three windows were broken, and there were two large stones on the floor. As they stood in the middle of the room, a third stone broke the third window.

'What's this?' said Adye.

'He's starting,' said Dr Kemp.

'Can he climb up the outside of the house?' asked Adye.

'It's impossible,' said Dr Kemp. 'Even a cat couldn't climb up there.'

'Do you have any shutters?' asked Adye.

'There are shutters downstairs, but not up here in my study,' said Dr Kemp.

There was a noise from downstairs.

'He's breaking the windows in the bedrooms now,' said Dr Kemp. 'But there are shutters there. The glass will fall outside and cut his feet.'

But downstairs the windows were breaking, one by one.

'I'll go down to the police station,' said Adye. 'We'll get some dogs. Have you got a stick or something like that?'

Another window broke.

'Do you have a gun?' asked Adye.

Dr Kemp's hand went to his pocket. 'I've only got this one,' he said, showing Adye. 'I think I need it.'

'I'll bring it back,' said Adye. 'You're safe here.'

Dr Kemp gave him the gun, and the two men went back downstairs.

'Now for the door,' said Adye.

The two men waited by the door for a minute. Then they heard a window break at the back of the house. Dr Kemp unlocked the door and opened it and Adye went outside. Dr Kemp closed the door immediately, and locked it.

Adye stood for a moment with his back to the door. Then he walked down the steps and through the garden in front of the house. Something moved the grass. Was it the wind?

'Stop!' said a Voice.

Adye stopped. His hand was on the gun in his pocket.

'Go back to the house,' said the Voice.

'Sorry,' said Adye. The Voice was in front of him, and to the left. Could he fire at it?

'Where are you going?' asked the Voice. Adye moved his hand on the gun. The sun caught the metal in his pocket.

'I can go where I want,' said Adye.

Immediately an arm came round his neck and he was pushed over. He took out the gun and fired – at nothing. Then the Invisible Man hit him in the mouth and took the gun from his hand.

The Voice laughed. 'I don't want to kill you now. I can only fire this gun four more times and I need to kill Kemp first.'

The gun was in the air, six feet away.

'Well?' asked Adye. 'What do you want?'

'Get up,' said the Voice. 'And don't try anything clever. Remember, I can see your face, but you can't see mine. You've got to go back in the house.'

'He won't let me in,' said Adye.

'He must,' said the Voice. 'I can't let you go. You must go back inside the house.'

'I'll try,' said Adye. 'But you must promise to stay outside in the garden.'

12

The End of the Game

Dr Kemp was still in his house. He was standing in the broken glass by the window in his study upstairs and trying to watch Adye in the garden. He could see that Adye was talking to someone. 'Why doesn't he fire?' he said to himself. Then he saw the gun.

'He's given the gun to the Invisible Man,' he said.

'Promise to stay outside,' said Adye again.

'You go back in the house,' said the Invisible Man. 'I won't promise anything.' He waved the gun dangerously.

Adye walked slowly back towards the house, his hands behind his back. Dr Kemp could see the gun behind him. Then things happened very quickly. Adye jumped backwards suddenly, turning, and reaching out for the gun. He did not catch it. Adye's hands went up in the air, and Dr Kemp heard the gun. Adye fell forwards onto his face, tried to push himself up, and then fell back. He did not move.

For a few minutes Dr Kemp stood at the window, looking down at Colonel Adye. Adye was lying on the grass, not moving. It was hot, and nothing was moving. Down the hill, Dr Kemp could see an old man asleep in his garden. How did he not wake up when he heard the gun? Dr Kemp looked around for the gun, but he could not see it anymore. His eyes turned back to Adye, who still did not move. The Invisible Man's game had started.

Suddenly the bell rang and someone started knocking angrily at the door. Then it was quiet again. Dr Kemp looked out of each of the three windows, then went to the top of the stairs and listened again. He picked up the poker from his bedroom, and went to check the shutters on all the windows downstairs. Everything seemed all right. He went back upstairs to his study. Adye was still on the grass. Dr Kemp's servant and two policemen were walking up the hill.

It was still very quiet. The three people seemed to move very slowly. 'What is the Invisible Man doing now?' thought Dr Kemp. He went downstairs again.

Suddenly he heard a terrible noise from the kitchen. He unlocked the door and went in. As he opened the door, the shutters broke and flew into the house. An axe[62] was hitting the shutters and the window. Then the axe fell on the ground and Dr Kemp saw his gun at the window. He ran back through the door. The Invisible Man fired, but he was a moment too late. Dr Kemp could hear the Invisible Man shouting and laughing. He closed and locked the kitchen door.

In a minute the Invisible Man would be in the kitchen. And the kitchen door would not hold for long, not against someone with an axe.

The front door bell rang. It was the two policemen and the servant. Dr Kemp let them in and then quickly locked the door again.

'It's the Invisible Man,' said Dr Kemp. 'He has a gun, and he can fire it twice more. I think he's killed Adye. Did you see him on the grass at the front of the house?'

'We came through the back garden,' said the servant.

'What's that noise?' asked the other policeman.

'He's in the kitchen – or he will be,' said Dr Kemp. 'He's got an axe –'

Then they heard the axe hitting the kitchen door. The servant saw the door moving, and ran into the dining room[63]. Dr Kemp and the policemen followed her.

'Here!' said Dr Kemp. He went to the fire and picked up two more pokers. He gave one to each of the policemen. The kitchen door flew open and they saw the axe and a gun. The Invisible Man fired the gun again, hitting a painting on the wall above Dr Kemp's head. One of the policemen brought his poker down on the gun and it fell to the floor. The axe was still in the air.

'Stand back, you two,' said the Invisible Man. 'I want Kemp.'

'We want you,' said one of the policemen, coming forward and waving his poker. The Invisible Man moved back quickly, and the policeman hit nothing. The Invisible Man hit back with the axe. It hit the policeman on the head, and he fell to the floor at the bottom of the stairs. The second policeman now hit out with his poker. He went for the Invisible Man's arm, just behind the axe, and he hit something soft. The Invisible Man shouted, and the axe fell to the floor. The policeman tried to hit him again, but there was nothing there. He put his foot on the axe and waited.

The other policeman sat up. He had blood on his face from a deep cut. 'Where is he?' he asked.

'I don't know,' said the second policeman. 'I hit him. He's still here, I think. Unless he's in the dining room. Dr Kemp?'

There was no answer.

The other policeman stood up. Then he heard the noise of the Invisible Man's feet. They went into the kitchen and towards the back door. He decided not to follow him, but to go into the dining room. 'Dr Kemp?' he said.

He stopped. The two policemen stood in the dining room door. The window was wide open. Dr Kemp and the servant had gone.

———

Mr Heelas, Dr Kemp's neighbour, was asleep in his garden when the attack began. Mr Heelas did not believe the stories about the Invisible Man. On summer days he always slept in the garden after lunch, and he was sleeping there today. His wife did believe the stories, and she was in the house. The breaking windows did not wake him up at first, but he did wake after a time. There was something different about Dr Kemp's house, he thought. And then he saw that every window was broken. And every window, except those at the top of the house, was closed with wooden shutters.

'That's strange,' he said to himself. 'Everything was fine twenty minutes ago.'

More glass was breaking. And then the shutters in the dining room window opened and Mr Kemp's servant climbed out. Dr Kemp himself followed her. Mr Heelas stood up to see things better. Dr Kemp ran around the house, through some trees. He started to climb over the wall between his garden and Mr Heelas's garden.

Mr Heelas suddenly had an idea. 'I say! Perhaps it's that Invisible Man. My wife was right!' He ran towards his house as fast as he could, shouting, 'Close the doors! Close the windows! The Invisible Man is coming!'

He ran in through the back door and locked it behind him. Dr Kemp was not far behind him, running across the grass. He ran up to the window of the living room, and Mr Heelas looked at him through the window in the door.

'I'm sorry,' said Mr Heelas, 'But you can't come in. I'm sorry if he's chasing you, but I can't open the door.'

Dr Kemp ran around the house to the front and onto the road. Mr Heelas, watching the garden, could see invisible feet running through his beautiful flowers.

Dr Kemp ran down the road towards Port Burdock. He was a young man and he ran quickly, but he soon started to get tired. It was much further to Port Burdock than he thought.

There was nobody else on the road, and all the houses were probably locked as the police had asked. And he could hear feet behind him on the road.

After a few minutes he was in the town and running towards the police station. There were people in the street here, and he shouted to warn them. More people came out into the street. Some of them were holding sticks.

'Stand across the road,' shouted one man with a large stick. 'Don't let him pass!'

'He's here,' shouted Dr Kemp. 'He's just behind me.'

'Aha!' shouted a Voice.

The Invisible Man hit Dr Kemp hard under the ear. Dr Kemp tried to hit back. Then the Invisible Man hit him again, in the face, and Dr Kemp fell to the ground. He felt two hands around his neck. He reached up and tried to catch the Invisible Man's arms. He did so, and the Invisible Man shouted. Then a man came up behind him and hit the Invisible Man hard with a stick. Dr Kemp felt the Invisible Man fall and held on to his arms tightly.

'I've got him,' he shouted. 'Help me! Hold him down! Hold his feet!'

Now two or three men were holding the Invisible Man. Sticks were flying and there was a lot of shouting. The Invisible Man seemed to stand up again, and then fell down heavily.

'He's hurt,' said Dr Kemp. 'Stand back!'

The men moved back. Dr Kemp was still holding the Invisible Man's arms.

'He's hurt,' said Dr Kemp again. 'His mouth's wet and … Oh, no!' There was blood on his hands.

His hands were on the Invisible Man's head now, and then they moved further down. 'I think he's dead,' he said.

'Look!' shouted an old woman.

Everybody was looking closely. They were now just beginning to see the Invisible Man's body. First, he looked like

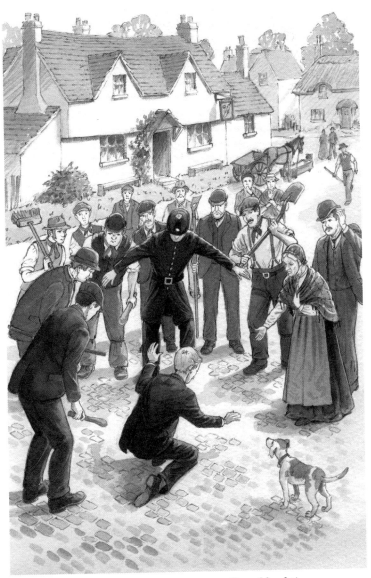

'He's hurt,' said Dr Kemp. 'Stand back!'

glass. They could see him, but they could see through him. Then they could see the hands and feet. And, after a minute or two, they could see the body of a young man of about thirty. His hair and beard were white, and his eyes were wide open and red.

Three children were pushing through the crowd, but somebody turned them around and sent them away. 'Put something over his face,' said one of the men.

Somebody brought a blanket out of the Jolly Cricketers and put it over him. They carried him in and put him in one of the bedrooms. And there, on an old bed in a cheap hotel, the Invisible Man's experiment ended.

13

The Story Ends

That is the end of the story of Griffin's experiment. If you want to know more about it you must go to a little pub in Port Stowe. Talk to the man who lives there. The name of the pub is The Invisible Man. And you know who lives there. He's fatter now, and he has got new boots. Buy something to eat or drink and he will tell you his story.

'I did quite well,' he will tell you. 'They didn't know where the money came from, so they said I could keep it. And then somebody gave me a job in the theatre. They paid me well and I told my story every night to crowds of people.'

You could ask him about the Invisible Man's diaries.

'Yes, I had them once,' he will say. 'But I don't have them anymore. That Dr Kemp in Port Burdock says that I have them, but he's wrong. The Invisible Man carried them off and hid them somewhere. I don't know where they are.'

He is not married, and he lives alone. He moves slowly because he is not a young man, and his life has been hard. He thinks a lot, and the people who live in Port Stowe think that he is very intelligent.

On Sunday mornings, and after ten o'clock in the evening, when the pub is closed, he goes quietly to his living room. He takes a key and opens a cupboard. There are three books inside. He takes them out and puts them on the table. They are old and green now, because they spent some time outside in bad weather. He sits down in his armchair and picks one of them up. He studies it carefully, turning the pages slowly.

'Oh, he was a clever man,' he says to himself. 'Full of secrets. Wonderful secrets.'

He turns the pages again. 'Yes,' he says. 'One day I'll understand it all. Of course, I won't make myself invisible, not at first.'

And Mr Marvel dreams. And although Dr Kemp has looked everywhere, and Colonel Adye has asked hundreds of people questions, only one man knows where to find the Invisible Man's wonderful diaries. And nobody else will know where they are, until he dies.

Points For Understanding

1

1 Why was Mrs Hall happy to have a new guest at the Coach and Horses?
2 Why did the stranger want to keep his coat and hat?
3 What reason did the stranger give to Mrs Hall for his visit?
4 Why did Teddy take a long time to work on the clock?

2

1 Why did the stranger run into the Coach and Horses when the dog bit him?
2 What did Mr Hall see when he followed the stranger into his room? What did he think about this?
3 What did the stranger do all afternoon?
4 Why did Dr Cuss visit the stranger? What happened when he was with him?

3

1 How did Mr and Mrs Bunting know that there was a burglar in the house?
2 Why did Mrs Hall not bring the stranger his food?
3 Why did Jaffers want to arrest the stranger?

4

1 Why did Mr Marvel not like either of his pairs of boots?
2 What did Dr Cuss and Mr Bunting find in the guests' lounge?
3 Why did the Invisible Man take Dr Cuss's clothes?

5

1 Did Mr Marvel want to help the Invisible Man?
2 Why did the old man in Port Stowe believe in the Invisible Man?
3 Why was Mr Marvel's pocket full of money?

6

1 Why did Dr Kemp not believe in the Invisible Man?
2 How did the Invisible Man get into the Jolly Cricketers?
3 How did the American try to stop the Invisible Man?

7

1 How did Dr Kemp find out that the Invisible Man was in his house?
2 What did Dr Kemp give the Invisible Man?
3 Why had the Invisible Man not had any sleep?
4 Did the Invisible Man think that he was safe with Dr Kemp? Why?
5 Why did Dr Kemp write to the Port Burdock police?

8

1 What were the most difficult parts of the body to make invisible?
2 What was the first living thing that Griffin tried to make invisible?
   What happened?
3 Why did Griffin have to become invisible quickly?
4 How could people see the Invisible Man in the street?

9

1 Why did the Invisible Man go to the department store?
2 What does the old man think is happening?
3 Why did the Invisible Man hit the old man on the head?
4 What did the Invisible Man take from the old man's shop?
5 Why could the Invisible Man not eat in a restaurant?

10

1 Why did the Invisible Man go to Port Burdock?
2 Why did the Invisible Man want to kill some people?
3 Why did Dr Kemp think that the Invisible Man was mad?
4 What plans did Dr Kemp suggest to Colonel Adye to help him catch the Invisible Man?

11

1 Why did Mr Wicksteed follow the Invisible Man?
2 Could the Invisible Man escape by train?
3 Why did Dr Kemp close all the shutters in his house?

12

1 How did the Invisible Man get into Dr Kemp's house?
2 Why did Mr Heelas not let Dr Kemp into his house?
3 What happened to the Invisible Man after he died?

13

1 What does Mr Marvel do every evening?

Glossary

1 **department store** (page 4)
a large shop that is divided into separate sections, with each section selling a different type of thing

2 **degree** (page 4)
the qualification that you get after completing a course of study at a university

3 **science fiction** (page 4)
books and films about imaginary future events that often include space travel and creatures from other planets

4 **base** – *to base something on something* (page 4)
to use something as a model for a film, piece of writing or work of art

5 **invisibility** (page 5)
something that is *invisible* cannot be seen. *Invisibility* is the fact of being invisible.

6 **invention** (page 5)
something that someone has made, designed or thought of for the first time, or the act of inventing something

7 **mostly** (page 5)
usually, most of the time or in most situations

8 **progress** (page 5)
the process of developing or improving

9 **research** (page 5)
the detailed study of something in order to discover new facts

10 **adaptation** (page 6)
a film or TV programme made from a book or play

11 **carrying** – *to carry something* (page 8)
to hold something using your hands, arms or body and take it somewhere

12 **glove** (page 8)
a piece of clothing that covers your hand and fingers

13 **shiny** (page 8)
something that is *shiny* has a bright surface that reflects light. If a person's nose is shiny, it usually means that they are cold or ill.

14 **landlady/landlord** (page 8)
a man or woman who owns or manages a pub or small hotel. Also someone who owns a house, flat or room that people can live in if they pay money.

15 **light** – *to light something* (page 8)
to make something such as a fire or lamp start to burn

16 **beard** (page 8)
hair that grows on a man's face – on his chin and cheeks

17 **knock** – *to knock on something* (page 10)
to hit a door with your hand or with a piece of metal called a knocker

18 **handkerchief** (page 10)
a small piece of cloth or paper that you use for wiping your nose, face or eyes

19 **bandage** (page 10)
a long thin piece of cloth that you wrap around an injured part of your body

20 **embarrassed** (page 10)
feeling slightly ashamed, and worried about what other people will think of you

21 **curtain** (page 10)
a long piece of cloth that hangs down to cover a window

22 **hurt** – *to hurt someone or something* (page 11)
to cause physical pain or injury to another person or to yourself

23 **relaxed** (page 11)
calm and not worried

24 **certainly** (page 11)
used for expressing agreement or for giving someone permission to do something

25 **experiment** (page 12)
a scientific test to find out what happens to someone or something in particular conditions

26 **immediately** (page 12)
very quickly and without delay

27 **cart** (page 13)
an open vehicle with four wheels that is pulled by a horse. Someone who drives a cart is called a *carter*.

28 **poison** (page 14)
a substance that can kill you or make you ill if you eat, drink or breathe it

29 **shilling** (page 15)
   a small unit of money that was used in the UK until 1971. In the time when Wells wrote *The Invisible Man*, this was a lot of money for Mrs Hall.

30 **vicar** (page 16)
   someone whose job is to perform religious duties and ceremonies in the Church of England

31 **burglary** (page 17)
   the crime of entering a building illegally in order to steal things. Someone who commits this crime is called a *burglar*.

32 **poker** (page 17)
   a metal stick for moving the coal and wood of a fire around

33 **study** (page 17)
   a room in a house where you can work or read quietly

34 **sneeze** (page 17)
   the loud sound a person makes when they blow air out of their nose in a sudden uncontrolled way, for example because they have a cold

35 **blanket** (page 19)
   a *blanket* is a a thick cover made of wool or another material that you use to keep warm in bed

36 **chase** – *to chase someone or something* (page 20)
   the action of following someone or something quickly because you want to stop them so that they cannot escape

37 **removed** – *to remove* (page 20)
   to take off clothes, or to take something away from a place

38 **arrest** – *to arrest someone* (page 21)
   if the police *arrest* someone they take that person to a police station because they think that he or she has committed a crime. The police use *handcuffs* – metal rings that are put round a person's wrists – to stop a prisoner from using their hands.

39 **mile** (page 22)
   a unit for measuring distance, equal to 1.609 kilometres

40 **anywhere** (page 23)
   used in a negative statement instead of 'somewhere'

41 **code** (page 23)
   a system of words, number or signs used for sending secret messages

42 **tablecloth** (page 24)
   a large cloth for covering a table

43 **foot** (page 24)

a foot is a unit used for measuring length, that is equal to 12 inches and equal to about 30 centimetres

44 **tightly** (page 25)

if you hold something *tightly* you hold it in a strong way

45 **bench** (page 25)

a hard seat for two or more people to sit on outside

46 **lie** (page 26)

something that you say or write that is not true and that you know is not true

47 **microscope** (page 27)

a piece of scientific equipment for looking at things that are too small to see normally

48 **breathing** – *to breathe* (page 27)

to take air into your lungs through your nose or mouth and let it out again

49 **murder** (page 28)

the crime of deliberately killing someone

50 **fire** – *to fire* (page 28)

if a gun, *fires* or someone *fires* it, someone uses it to shoot someone

51 **servant** (page 30)

someone whose job is to cook, clean or do other work in someone else's home

52 **albino** (page 32)

a person or animal who has very pale skin, white hair or fur and pink eyes because of a medical condition they were born with

53 **drug** (page 35)

a substance that you take to treat a disease or medical problem

54 **step** (page 40)

a flat surface, usually one in a series, that you walk up or down in order to move to a different level

55 **wig** (page 44)

a cover of artificial – not real – hair that you wear on your head

56 **mask** (page 45)

something that you wear to cover all or part of your face

57 **interrupted** – *to interrupt* (page 50)

to say or do something that stops someone when they are speaking or thinking about something

58 **got away** – *to get away from someone or something* (page 52)

to escape from a person or place

59 *inch* (page 53)
   a unit for measuring how long something is. An *inch* is equal to 2.54 centimetres.
60 *shutter* (page 55)
   a cover that can be closed over the inside or outside of a window. Dr Kemp's *shutters* are on the inside of the windows.
61 *attacked* – *to attack someone or something* (page 55)
   to use physical force to hurt people or damage property
62 *axe* (page 59)
   a tool used for cutting wood. It has a long wooden handle and a heavy sharp metal blade for cutting
63 *dining room* (page 60)
   the room in a house or hotel where you eat meals

Useful Phrases

on the run (page 16)
trying to hide or escape from the police

make them jump – *to make someone jump* (page 39)
to make someone very surprised and make them move their body
slightly because of this

on your side – to be on someone's side (page 50)
if someone is on another person's side, they want them to win in an
argument or fight. Dr Kemp wants to tell people the true story about
the Invisible Man so that people will understand and want to help him.

Glossary and Useful Phrases definitions adapted from the Macmillan Essential Dictionary © *Macmillan Publishers Limited 2003* www.macmillandictionary.com

Exercises

Background Information

Read 'A Note About The Author' and 'A Note About The Story'.
Write T (True) or F (False).

1   H.G. Wells was born in 1686.   _F_

2   He had four brothers and sisters.   ....

3   He started reading a lot when he broke his leg.   ....

4   *The Time Machine* was the first book he published.   ....

5   In the 1930s people could listen to H.G. Wells talking   ....
    on the radio.

6   The story is set in the future.   ....

7   The story only looks at the good points of being invisible.   ....

8   The story has been made into a film a number of times.   ....

Events in the Story

Put these events in the correct order.

a) A strange man arrives at the Coach and Horses. `1`

b) Dr Cuss takes off his clothes and gives them to the Invisible Man.

c) Dr Cuss visits the stranger at the Coach and Horses.

d) Dr Kemp tells Colonel Adye about the Invisible Man and the diaries.

e) People start to be able to see the Invisible Man again. First his hands and feet can be seen, and then the rest of his body.

f) The American tries to shoot the Invisible Man.

g) The Invisible Man chases Dr Kemp down the street and is caught by a crowd of people.

h) The Invisible Man tells Dr Kemp about his experiments.

i) The Invisible Man visits Dr Kemp late at night.

j) The police start searching for the Invisible Man.

k) There is a burglary at the vicar's house.

l) There is a story in the newspaper about the Invisible Man.

Multiple Choice

Tick the best answer.

1 What did Mrs Hall think was wrong with the stranger?
   a He was hiding something.
   b He had had an accident. ✓
   c The police were looking for him.
   d He felt very cold.

2 Why did the policeman want to arrest the stranger?
   a Because he was a burglar
   b Because he was invisible
   c Because he had not paid his bill
   d Because he was running away from the police

3 Who agreed to help the Invisible Man?
   a Dr Cuss
   b Mr Bunting
   c Mr Hall
   d Mr Marvel

4 What did Mr Marvel tell the old man on the bench?
   a That there was a story in the newspaper about an Invisible Man.
   b That he did not know anything about the Invisible Man.
   c That he had been in Iping.
   d That he had lots of money in his pocket.

5 Which of these people was not in the Jolly Cricketers pub?
   a An American
   b Dr Kemp
   c A taxi driver
   d A policeman

6 What did Dr Kemp do after he spoke to the Invisible Man?
   a He gave the Invisible Man something to eat.
   b He tried to phone the police.
   c He tried to run away.
   d He went to sleep because he was tired.

7 Which part of the Invisible Man's body could the boys see?
  a His eyes
  b His hair
  c His hands
  d His feet

8 What did the Invisible Man take with him when he left the department store?
  a Nothing
  b Some food
  c Some clothes
  d A blanket

9 Who thinks of a plan to catch the Invisible Man?
  a Colonel Adye
  b Dr Kemp
  c Mr Marvel
  d A policeman

10 Who did the Invisible Man kill?
  a Colonel Adye
  b Dr Kemp
  c Mr Marvel
  d Mr Wicksteed

11 How did Dr Kemp get out of his house?
  a He ran out of the back door.
  b He climbed out of a window.
  c He ran out of the front door.
  d He didn't. He stayed in his study.

12 What happened to the Invisible Man's diaries at the end of the story?
  a They were lost forever.
  b The police kept them.
  c Dr Kemp found them and read them.
  d Mr Marvel kept them locked in a cupboard.

Vocabulary: Letter fills

Complete each space with a letter to make a word from the story.

1 Mrs Hall looked at the stranger and felt _e_ mb_a_ rras _s_ e _d_.

2 The poor man must have had an accident and _____rt himself.

3 There was a loud s__ee____ but they could not see anyone in the room.

4 The stranger jumped up suddenly and began to c__a__e Mrs Hall around the room.

5 'It's not a crime to be invisible, so why do you want to ___rr__s___ me?' the stranger said.

6 'He could be an_____h__r__, he's invisible,' he said.

7 An old man sat down on the __en____ next to him and started reading a newspaper.

8 Suddenly there was a loud __no__k on the door.

9 'You can't shoot him,' the policeman said, 'That's m__r__e__!'

10 He ran up the _____e__s from the street and went inside the house.

Word Focus

Complete the sentences with one of the words from the box.

> bandage   code   experiments   ~~invisible~~   lie
> poison   removed   shiny   tightly   wig

1 The stranger was in the room, but Jaffers could not see him because he was _____*invisible*_____.

2 Scientists like Dr Kemp often do _____ to find out new things.

3 The stranger put on some glasses, gloves and a _____ that looked just like real hair.

4 The old man did not believe the story. He thought it was a _____.

5 First he took off his hat and his beard and then he _____ all of his clothes.

6 The Invisible Man held Mr Marvel's arm _____ and said, 'If you try to run away again, I'll kill you.'

7 Mrs Hall looked at the stranger. All of his face was covered by a _____ and he was wearing dark glasses.

8 They tried to read the books, but they could not understand anything as it was all written in _____.

9 The stranger's nose was very _____.

10 Some of the bottles contained _____ that would kill anyone who drank it.

Useful Words and Phrases

Match the words on the left with a word on the right to make a compound word or phrase from the story.

1	on the	a	jump
2	on your	b	fiction
3	department	c	run
4	get	d	room
5	make someone	e	store
6	dining	f	away
7	science	g	side

Match the words or phrases above to their meaning below.

1 trying to hide or escape from the police ....1......

2 books and films about imaginary future events that often include space travel ....

3 to surprise someone so that they move slightly because of this ....

4 the room in a house or a hotel where you eat a meal ....

5 a large shop that is divided into separate sections that sell different things ....

6 to escape from a person or a place ....

7 to want someone to win an argument or a fight; to support someone ....

Grammar: Modal verbs

Choose the correct modal verb to complete each sentence.

1 It is in the newspaper so it (must) / would be true.

2 Teddy told Mr Hall that he should not / would not want a man like that in his house.

3 'Today the weather is good, but tomorrow it can / may rain and then we'll find him,' said the policeman.

4 'I've had an accident and I could / have to be careful with my eyes,' said the stranger.

5 She could / must hear a noise, but there was nothing there.

6 The story has to / will be in all the newspapers tomorrow.

7 'I'm sorry, but I can't / wouldn't help you,' said Mr Marvel.

8 'We might / must catch him before he escapes,' said Dr Kemp.

9 With an axe it must / would only take him a minute to get through the kitchen door.

10 'You couldn't / won't believe this, but it's true,' he told the old man.

Grammar: Dependent prepositions

Choose the correct preposition to complete the sentences.

1 'I'll kill you if you try .... run away again,' said the Invisible Man.
   a about   **b** for   (**c** to)

2 Luckily for the Invisible Man, the dog was interested .... the music
   and left him alone.
   a about   **b** for   **c** in

3 Mrs Hall asked .... two pounds and the stranger paid her.
   a about   **b** for   **c** in

4 Dr Kemp was a man of science and he did not believe .... invisible
   people.
   a about   **b** in   **c** with

5 'I was really angry .... him, so I hit him on the head,' said the
   Invisible Man.
   a for   **b** in   **c** with

6 People in the village could not agree .... the stranger. Some
   thought he was a scientist and others thought he was hiding.
   a about   **b** for   **c** in

7 The Invisible Man was standing outside waiting .... Mr Marvel to
   come out.
   a about   **b** for   **c** to

Grammar: Time expressions

Complete each sentence with a time expression from the box. Use each expression only once.

> a few minutes later   a long time   afternoon   As soon as   at any time
> every week   in early February   Most days   Several times   the next day

1 Mrs Hall was happy when the stranger arrived, as it was rare to have visitors with money _____*at any time*_____ and especially in winter.

2 The Invisible Man stayed in his room and worked all
_____.

3 The Invisible Man had arrived in Iping _____ when the snow was falling.

4 At the start of his stay he paid his bills _____ and Mrs Hall was happy.

5 _____ Mrs Hall heard strange noises coming from the stranger's room.

6 The door slammed shut, but _____ they heard it opening and the stranger came downstairs.

7 For _____ Dr Kemp stood at the window and looked down the road.

8 I stayed in the store until _____ and when they opened the doors I heard people coming in.

9 _____ the boxes were in his room he started opening them and taking out lots of bottles.

10 _____ in the summer Mr Heelas slept in his garden after lunch.

Pronunciation: Word stress

Match the words to the correct stress pattern.

arrest   ● ●

information   ● ●

certainly   ● ● ●

progress (noun)   ● ● ●

tomorrow   ● ● ● ●

Visit the Macmillan Readers website at www.macmillanenglish.com/readers

*to find **FREE resources** for use in class and for independent learning. Search our **online catalogue** to buy new Readers including **audio download** and **eBook** versions.*

Here's a taste of what's available:

For the classroom:

- **Tests** for most Readers to check understanding and monitor progress
- **Worksheets** for most Readers to explore language and themes
- **Listening worksheets** to practise extensive listening
- Worksheets to help prepare for the **First (FCE) reading exam**

Additional resources for students and independent learners:

- An **online level test** to identify reading level
- **Author information sheets** to provide in-depth biographical information about our Readers authors
- **Self-study worksheets** to help track and record your reading which can be used with any Reader
- Use our **creative writing worksheets** to help you write short stories, poetry and biographies
- Write academic essays and literary criticism confidently with the help of our **academic writing worksheets**
- Have fun completing our **webquests** and **projects** and learn more about the Reader you are studying
- Go backstage and read **interviews** with **famous authors** and **actors**
- Discuss your favourite Readers at the **Book Corner Club**

Visit www.macmillanenglish.com/readers to find out more!

Macmillan Education
4 Crinan Street
London N1 9XW
A division of Macmillan Publishers Limited
Companies and representatives throughout the world

ISBN 978-0-230-46032-4
ISBN 978-0-230-46033-1 (with CD edition)

The Invisible Man by H. G. Wells

First published 2014

Designed by Carolyn Gibson
Illustrated by John Dillow
Cover photograph by **Getty Images/David Hanover**

Printed and bound in Thailand

without CD edition

2019   2018   2017   2016   2015   2014
10   9   8   7   6   5   4   3   2   1

with CD edition

2019   2018   2017   2016   2015   2014
10   9   8   7   6   5   4   3   2   1